DS

DESERT FOOD CHAINS

Buffy Silverman

www.raintreepublishers.co.uk
Visit our website to find out
more information about
Raintree books.

To order:
☎ Phone 0845 6044371
▤ Fax +44 (0) 1865 312263
✉ Email myorders@raintreepublishers.co.uk

Customers from outside the UK please telephone +44 1865 312262

Raintree is an imprint of Capstone Global Library Limited,
a company incorporated in England and Wales having its
registered office at 7 Pilgrim Street, London, EC4V 6LB
– Registered company number: 6695582

Edited by Abby Colich and Andrew Farrow
Designed by Victoria Allen
Illustrated by Words and Publications
Picture research by Mica Brancic
Originated by Capstone Global Library Ltd
Printed by China Translation & Printing Services Ltd

ISBN 978 0 431 01379 4 (hardback)
14 13 12 11 10
10 9 8 7 6 5 4 3 2 1

British Library Cataloguing in Publication Data
Silverman, Buffy.
Desert food chains. -- (Protecting food chains)
577.5'416-dc22
A full catalogue record for this book is available from the
British Library.

Acknowledgments
The author and publisher are grateful to the following for
permission to reproduce copyright material: Alamy pp. **31**
(© Mike Lane), **43** (© Jim Parkin); FLPA p. **42** (Imagebroker/
Norbert Eisele-Hei); Getty Images p. **14** (Workbook
Stock/Brenda Tharp); Photolibrary pp. **4** (age fotostock/
John Cancalosi), **8** (age fotostock/Gonzalo Azumendi), **9**
(WaterFrame - Underwater Images/Daniela Dirscherl), **13**
(Oxford Scientific (OSF)/Olivier Grunewald), **15** (Oxford
Scientific (OSF)/John Netherton), **17** (F1 Online/M
Schaef), **18** (Ambient Images/Richard Wong), **19** (Juniors
Bildarchiv), **21** (Animals Animals/Hans & Judy Beste), **22**
(Animals Animals/Joe McDonald), **23** (Animals Animals/CC.
Lockwood), **26** (Cusp/Theo Allofs), **27** (Oxford Scientific
(OSF)/Elliott Neep), **29** (age fotostock/Bruno Morandi), **33**
(age fotostock/Pablo H. Caridad), **34** (SGM SGM), **35** (arabian
Eye/Kami Kami), **37** (Chris McLennan), **38** (Index Stock
Imagery/Mark Segal), **39** (Picture Press/Berndt Fischer), **40**
(Ted Mead), **41** (age fotostock/Nigel Dennis); Shutterstock pp.
25 (Oksana Perkins), **36** (© J. Matzick).

Cover photograph of a rattlesnake ready to strike reproduced
with permission of Photolibrary (Index Stock Imagery/Gary
McVicker).

Cover and spread background image reproduced with
permission of Shutterstock (© Amir Hossein Biparva).

We would like to thank Kenneth Dunton and Dana Sjostrom
for their invaluable help in the preparation of this book.

Every effort has been made to contact copyright holders
of any material reproduced in this book. Any omissions
will be rectified in subsequent printings if notice is given
to the publisher.

CONTENTS

Words appearing in bold, **like this**, are explained in the glossary.

WHAT IS A DESERT FOOD CHAIN?

Imagine a desert scene. You might expect sand as far as you can see, with no living creatures. Deserts are the driest places on Earth, and they can be very hot or very cold. But there is more to deserts than vast areas of sand. Deserts are home to plants and animals that live nowhere else on Earth. These plants and animals have **adapted** to life with little water.

Picture the Kalahari Desert of Africa. Desert grasses take in **energy** from the Sun and use it to make food. Dune crickets get their energy by chewing on desert grasses. The crickets, in turn, are food for meerkats. When grasses, crickets, and meerkats die, **bacteria** break down the dead bodies. The flow of energy from grass, to cricket, to meerkat, and to bacteria is called a food chain.

A desert tortoise gets energy from eating flowers and other plants.

READING A FOOD CHAIN

A food chain diagram shows how energy flows in a **habitat**. The arrows show the direction that energy and **nutrients** travel in the chain. For example, the spinifex hopping mouse gets energy from grass. The falcon gets energy from the mouse, and so on. All living things need energy to live and grow. They get energy from food, just like you get energy when you eat. Plants and animals are connected to one another by the flow of energy.

If something happens to one **organism** in a desert food chain, it affects the entire food chain. Humans have done many things to harm desert food chains, but we depend on them, too. That is why it is important to protect them.

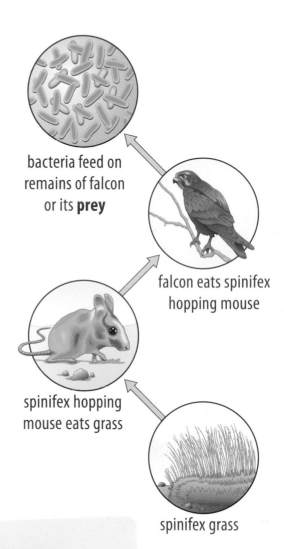

bacteria feed on remains of falcon or its **prey**

falcon eats spinifex hopping mouse

spinifex hopping mouse eats grass

spinifex grass

This diagram shows how energy flows from one organism to another in an Australian desert food chain.

WHAT ARE THE PARTS OF A FOOD CHAIN?

A typical food chain links four organisms in a habitat: a **producer**, a **primary consumer**, a **secondary consumer**, and a **decomposer**.

The food chain starts with a producer. Green plants are producers. A producer makes its own food using the Sun's energy. This process is called **photosynthesis**.

The next link in a food chain is an animal that eats a producer. It might be a hummingbird that sips **nectar** from a flower, a camel that **grazes** on leaves, or a beetle that chews seeds. All of these animals are **herbivores**, or animals that eat plants. Herbivores are also called primary consumers. They get energy by feeding on producers.

Animals that eat other animals are called secondary consumers. This is the next link in the food chain. A lizard that eats a beetle is a secondary consumer. **Consumers** can be **carnivores**, animals that eat only animals. They can also be **omnivores**, animals that eat plants and animals.

Over time, all living organisms die. Then, organisms called decomposers break down dead plants and animals. A decomposer returns nutrients to the food chain.

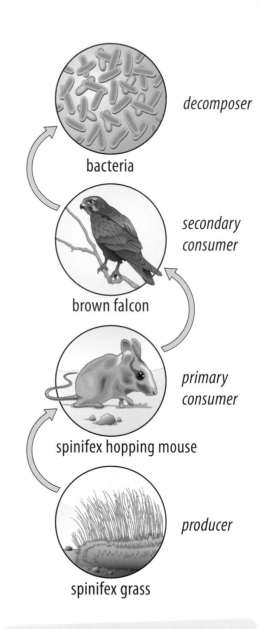

decomposer

bacteria

secondary consumer

brown falcon

primary consumer

spinifex hopping mouse

producer

spinifex grass

In this Australian desert food chain, energy flows from producers, to consumers, to decomposers.

WHAT IS A FOOD WEB?

Different food chains in the same habitat can be connected in a food web. A food chain follows a single path. It shows the flow of energy and nutrients along that chain. However, in nature, many organisms eat the same food. A food web is made of many linked food chains. It shows the different paths that energy and nutrients can travel.

The arrows in a food web show the flow of energy and nutrients from producers, to primary consumers, to secondary consumers, and to decomposers.

This is a food web diagram of the Australian desert. Arrows lead from spinifex grass to the animals that consume the grass – ants, bilbies, and spinifex hopping mice.

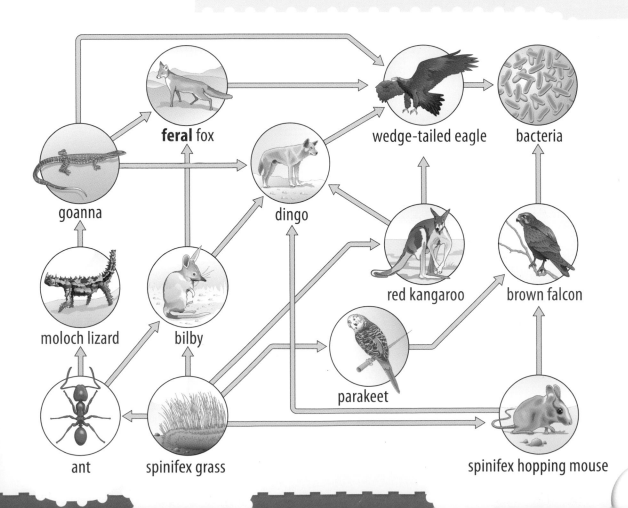

feral fox

wedge-tailed eagle   bacteria

goanna

dingo

red kangaroo   brown falcon

moloch lizard   bilby

parakeet

ant   spinifex grass   spinifex hopping mouse

WHAT IS A DESERT HABITAT?

A desert is a **habitat** with little rainfall. Not all deserts are covered with sand. Some have sandy soil scattered with pebbles and rocks. Others have rocky mountains.

Whether it is sandy or rocky, a desert is **arid** (dry). Less than 25 centimetres (10 inches) of rain falls each year. In some deserts, there is no rain for an entire year or longer. Then there may be heavy rains that flood the land. In other deserts, small amounts of rain fall throughout the year.

Plants that grow in the Atacama Desert of Chile are adapted to survive with little water.

A fennec fox's ears are adapted to help it hear its **prey** from far away. They also release heat to help the fox keep cool.

DESERT ADAPTATIONS

Deserts can be very cold or very hot. All deserts are places with little rainfall. This lack of rainfall makes deserts a tough place for plants and animals to survive in. Those that live in deserts have developed **adaptations** that help them to survive. Many are able to go for long periods without water, for example.

WHERE IN THE WORLD ARE DESERT HABITATS?

This map shows some of the main deserts of the world.

NORTH AMERICA

Mojave Desert

Sonoran Desert

SOUTH AMERICA

Atacama Desert

Patagonian Desert

Kara-Kum
Desert

ASIA

EUROPE

Takla Makan
Desert

Gobi Desert

Iranian Desert

Sahara Desert *AFRICA*

Arabian Desert

Namib Desert

Kalahari Desert

Australian
Deserts

AUSTRALIA

ANTARCTICA

WHAT ARE THE PRODUCERS IN DESERTS?

At first it may not seem like there are many plants in the desert. Take a closer look, however, and you will find many types of desert **producer**. Like all producers, these plants use the Sun's **energy** to make food. They do this using **photosynthesis**. Plants take in **nutrients** from the ground. They are the first link in a desert food chain.

Desert plants are **adapted** to survive with little water. They have thick leaves and stems to reduce water loss from **evaporation**. Some desert plants store water after a rainstorm. Others reach water with deep roots. Still others wait for rain and then grow quickly.

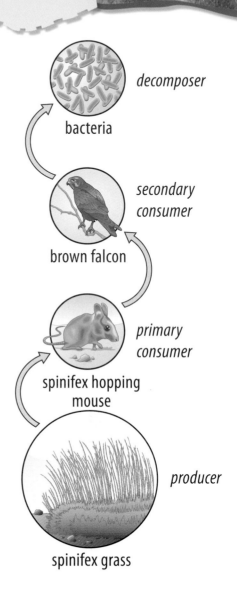

decomposer

bacteria

secondary consumer

brown falcon

primary consumer

spinifex hopping mouse

producer

spinifex grass

LOSING A LINK: CACTI

Many gardeners grow cacti. Where do these plants come from? Some are grown in nurseries, but sometimes people dig up wild cacti. When too many plants are collected, cacti become rare. This harms birds, insects, and other animals that depend on cacti for food, water, and shelter. In many places, laws protect cacti. If you buy a cactus, ask if it was grown from seed in a nursery.

Producers are the first link in a desert food chain. Producers are plants that use the Sun's energy to make food.

A saguaro cactus grows as large as a tree. During rainstorms, its roots suck up water and store it inside its thick stem. Sharp spines stop some animals from chewing to reach the water inside.

STORING WATER

Some desert plants, such as cacti, are adapted to store water. Most plants lose water through their leaves. Cacti do not have leaves like other plants, but instead have tiny leaves at the base of their stems. Instead of using these leaves to make food, cacti photosynthesize in their green stems.

Saguaro cacti grow in the Sonoran Desert in the south-western United States and parts of Mexico. The saguaro stores water in its stem. Its roots extend in many directions and quickly take in water during rainstorms. The **pleated** (folded) stem of the cactus expands to hold water. During dry periods, the cactus uses its stored water, and the pleats contract.

During long droughts, mesquite trees drop their leaves so water does not evaporate out of them.

GROWING DEEP

Some plants adapt to dry desert life by growing a long **tap root**. The tap root reaches water far below the surface.

A mesquite is a small tree that grows in the deserts of South and North America. A mesquite's tap root can grow 45 to 60 metres (150 to 200 feet) below ground. Live roots of mesquite have been found in copper mines more than 50 metres (160 feet) below the surface. During a drought, a mesquite draws water from deep underground.

A mesquite also gets water through side roots that extend far from its trunk. These roots absorb water from a wide area after it rains. The tree's small leaves have a waxy coating that slows water loss from evaporation.

WAITING FOR RAIN

Some plants appear to be dead during drought, only to spring to life after a rain. Ocotillo grows in North American deserts. During a drought, it looks like dead sticks. But the plant is not dead. It grows new leaves after a rainstorm. Then it quickly blooms and sets seed. During a dry period, ocotillo sheds its leaves and stops growing. An ocotillo plant can do this six or more times in a year.

Other plants survive dry weather by sprouting from seeds after a heavy rain. Tumbleweed plants grow in the Sahara and Negev deserts of northern Africa and the Middle East. After the rainy season, a tumbleweed drops its leaves, curls up into a tight ball of branches, and dies. The ball rolls in the wind, carrying fruits in its centre. When it rains, the ball uncurls and the fruits open, dropping seeds. The seeds sprout in a few hours and quickly grow.

After a rainstorm, many desert plants grow leaves, flowers, and seeds.

WHAT ARE THE PRIMARY CONSUMERS IN DESERTS?

Energy and **nutrients** flow from plants to **primary consumers** in a desert food chain. Desert **producers** support many different types of **consumer**. A primary consumer in the desert might eat seeds, **graze** on plants, or sip **nectar** from flowers. Like all desert **organisms**, these primary consumers are **adapted** to survive with little water.

SEEKING SEEDS

After a rainstorm, desert plants flower and produce seeds. Many primary consumers eat seeds. Harvester ants that live in deserts around the world depend on seeds. Worker ants collect seeds and carry them back to their nest. Other workers take off the seeds' hard outer husks. Then they stash the seeds in an inner chamber. Workers crush seeds and mix them with saliva before feeding them to larvae.

Birds, mice, and other desert rodents also eat seeds in a desert. Certain desert mice, including Australian spinifex hopping mice, do not need to drink water. They get all the water they need from the seeds and other food they eat.

decomposer

bacteria

secondary consumer

brown falcon

primary consumer

spinifex hopping mouse

producer

spinifex grass

Primary consumers get their energy by eating seeds, flowers, or leaves in a desert food chain.

FINDING FLOWERS

Desert flowers bloom after rainstorms. The blooms attract **pollinators**. These animals carry **pollen** from flower to flower, helping plants to make seeds. Insects, birds, and bats all feed on pollen and nectar from desert flowers.

Rodents such as mice and gerbils can pollinate plants, too. Some **species** of hairy-footed gerbil live in a southern African desert called the Succulent Karoo, an area with an amazing diversity of plants and animals. The gerbils leave their burrows at night to find food. They visit a desert lily. The lily's flowers make thick, syrupy nectar. The gerbils push open flowers with their front legs to slurp nectar. When the gerbils visit another flower, they unintentionally pollinate it.

Gerbils drink nectar from lilies growing close to the ground. Pollen from the lilies sticks to their snouts.

Bighorn sheep get most of the water they need from the plants they eat.

GRAZING GREENERY

Many animals graze on the leaves and stems of desert plants. Jackrabbits in North American deserts chew grasses, twigs, the bark of shrubs, and cacti. During the heat of the day, jackrabbits rest under bushes. A jackrabbit's large ears help it to get rid of excess heat. Jackrabbits look for food at night, when it is cooler.

Bighorn sheep live in the deserts of the south-western United States and Mexico. They climb rocky mountains that rise up from desert plains. There, they graze on grasses, tough plants, shrubs, and cacti. In the winter, they get all the water they need from their food. In the summer, the sheep stay near water holes to drink every few days. They rest in caves or under cliffs on hot days. People have moved into the sheep's **habitat**, used water sources for livestock, and changed the land. As a result, the population of desert bighorn sheep has become **endangered**.

PROTECTING A LINK: ARABIAN ORYX

The Arabian oryx is an antelope that once roamed sandy Arabian deserts. Herds of oryx survived on hot, dry sand dunes and stony plains. These areas often had no rain for several years. The animal's white coat reflects the sun, helping it survive in the hot desert. Hunters prized the oryx's unusual coat and long horns. Using four-wheel drive vehicles and automatic weapons, people hunted oryx until they were almost **extinct**. By 1972, there were no oryx in the wild.

Oryx that had been bred in zoos were brought back into the wild, starting in 1982. There are now herds of wild oryx in Oman, Saudi Arabia, Israel, and Jordan.

Oryx herds follow the rain to find food, travelling many kilometres at night.

WHAT ARE THE SECONDARY CONSUMERS IN DESERTS?

Secondary consumers are **predators** that hunt animals. They can be **omnivores** that eat both plants and animals, or **carnivores** that eat only other animals. In a food chain, **energy** and **nutrients** captured by plants flow to **primary consumers**. When a primary consumer is eaten, some of its energy and nutrients become part of secondary consumers.

INSECT EATERS

Desert insects are a favourite food of many desert **consumers**. Spiders, toads, lizards, birds, and other animals all feast on insects.

The gila woodpecker eats beetles, grasshoppers, and ants, as well as the fruits and berries that it finds in North American deserts. With its long beak, a gila woodpecker drills a hole in a saguaro cactus or a desert tree. Inside a cactus it finds a cool, moist place to build a nest.

decomposer

bacteria

secondary consumer

brown falcon

primary consumer

spinifex hopping mouse

producer

spinifex grass

Secondary consumers hunt insects and other small animals that live in a desert.

A barking spider hunts animals that wander near it, including small birds.

Barking spiders are large, hairy tarantulas that hunt in Australian deserts. These spiders dig burrows under rocks or logs, where it is moist. From the entrance of its burrow, a barking spider catches insects, frogs, lizards, and mice. In the spring, when rains come, its burrow may flood. The hairs on the spider's body trap air bubbles, stopping it from drowning. When a larger predator approaches, a barking spider hisses.

An Australian desert lizard called the thorny devil can eat thousands of ants in a day. The lizard's body acts as a water collector. At night, dew forms and collects on its bumpy skin. The dew runs along grooves between its spines and flows to the lizard's mouth. When it rains, a thorny devil can suck in water from all parts of its body.

The desert horned viper is hidden from eagles and other predators when it buries itself in the sand.

HUNTERS IN THE DESERT

Many kinds of snake live in deserts. Like all reptiles, snakes need warmth to be active. However, deserts are often too warm. The desert horned viper lives in northern Africa and the Middle East. It buries itself in the sand by rapidly moving sideways. Sand keeps it cool during the day. At night it hunts lizards, rodents, and other small **mammals**. During cold winters, many desert snakes **hibernate** in burrows.

RUNNING FOR FOOD

Although a roadrunner can fly, this desert bird usually runs to catch a meal. It runs at speeds of up to 24 kilometres (15 miles) per hour. That is fast enough to catch a moving rattlesnake. A roadrunner grabs the snake by the tail and whips its head against the ground. Then it swallows its **prey**. A roadrunner also eats insects, spiders, mice, birds, and lizards. To save water, a roadrunner has a special gland on its beak that gets rid of extra salt. Because of this gland, it does not lose body water like other birds.

LOSING A LINK: DESERT TORTOISES

Ravens are successful hunters that live in many **habitats**. They thrive when they live near people, because they find food, water, and nesting places. With more and more people living near the Mojave Desert in North America, the raven population has grown.

Desert tortoises have lived in the Mojave Desert for millions of years. There are now few tortoises left in the desert because people have changed the tortoise's habitat. In addition, ravens prey on young tortoises and tortoise eggs, so few young tortoises survive. People are now trying to remove flocks of ravens where tortoises breed.

Ravens hunt young desert tortoises and tortoise eggs. Because there are so few desert tortoises left in the Mojave Desert, they are protected by law.

WHAT ARE THE DECOMPOSERS IN DESERTS?

Decomposers are an important link in every food chain. Without them, deserts would be littered with dead matter and wastes. Decomposers break down dead plants and animals. They use the **energy** and **nutrients** that remain in dead matter. They break matter down into smaller bits and release nutrients into the soil. Plants take up and use these nutrients when they grow in soil.

BACTERIA AND FUNGI

Bacteria live in every **habitat** on Earth. They are found in plants, animals, and soil. Bacteria are too small to see without a microscope. Millions and millions of them grow on dead plants and animals. As they grow and reproduce, bacteria release nutrients into the soil.

Fungi also help break down dead plants and animals. Many fungi need moisture and cannot grow in the desert. Certain fungi, however, are part of the thin **soil crust** in a desert. The living **organisms** in the soil crust hold in moisture and stop desert soil from **eroding**. They also recycle nutrients so plants can grow.

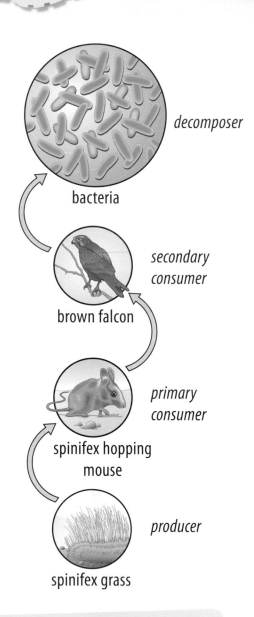

decomposer

bacteria

secondary consumer

brown falcon

primary consumer

spinifex hopping mouse

producer

spinifex grass

Decomposers are the final link in a food chain. They break down plants and animals.

Bacteria and fungi release chemicals called **enzymes** on to dead matter. Enzymes break down matter into smaller pieces that dissolve in water. Bacteria or fungi take in these dissolved pieces. They use the food energy to live and grow. Some of the nutrients become part of the soil.

LOSING A LINK: HARMING DECOMPOSERS

In many places, people are trying to limit where vehicles can drive in the desert. When a vehicle drives through the desert, its tyres press down and destroy the thin soil crust where bacteria and fungi live. Without these decomposers, nutrients no longer return to the soil. The soil erodes, and plants cannot grow.

Every time a vehicle drives through a desert habitat, it harms important decomposers.

SCAVENGERS: NATURE'S CLEAN-UP CREW

Scavengers are animals that feed on dead matter. While eating, they tear dead plants and animals into smaller pieces. Decomposers can break down these pieces and release nutrients.

TERMITES

A rotting log in a forest is often covered with fungi. But fungi need moisture, so few live on desert trees. Instead, termites break down dead trees and grasses. They grind up **cellulose** (the tough part of wood) with their jaws. Tiny organisms in a termite's gut can digest cellulose.

Termites live in colonies in deserts. Inside their nests, they store bits of dead grasses and trees for food. The colonies can be up to 1.5 metres (5 feet) tall.

LOSING A LINK: LAPPET-FACED VULTURE

Storks and vultures are important scavengers in the desert. They help break down dead animals by tearing them apart and feeding on them. Their bald heads and bare necks make it easier for them to reach into **carcasses**.

The lappet-faced vulture is the largest and most powerful vulture in Africa. With its strong beak, it can rip through the tough hides and muscles of large animals. Then smaller animals can feed on a carcass.

The number of lappet-faced vultures has slowly been declining. Some are poisoned by farmers who want to kill predators. Others are killed by people who mistakenly think vultures kill cattle. Many have disappeared because their habitat has been changed. People build homes where the vultures once lived and cut down trees where they built their nests.

A lappet-faced vulture chases away smaller vultures from a carcass.

DESERT MILLIPEDES

In hot deserts, millipedes are mostly active at night. They feed on decaying leaves and plants. During the daytime, a millipede stays underground in its burrow. If a **predator** bothers a millipede, it curls up in a ball. It gives off a bad-smelling chemical that irritates the predator's eyes and skin. Desert millipedes can live for 10 years and grow longer than your hand.

WHAT ARE DESERT FOOD CHAINS LIKE AROUND THE WORLD?

Deserts across the world are dry places. But every desert is unique, with different plants, animals, and **decomposers**. Hot deserts have different plants to moderate or cold deserts. The amount and timing of rainfall affects what grows in a desert.

SONORAN DESERT

North America's Sonoran Desert covers parts of Arizona and California in the US, and north-west Mexico. This large, hot desert is home to many unusual **producers**. Saguaro cacti grow only in the Sonoran Desert. Other cacti like prickly pear and organ pipe grow here. So do desert wild flowers.

The pig-like javelina eats mostly plants. Small groups of javelinas roam together in the desert. Juicy prickly-pear fruits help them survive when there is little water. **Secondary consumers** like coyotes, bobcats, and mountain lions **prey** on javelinas.

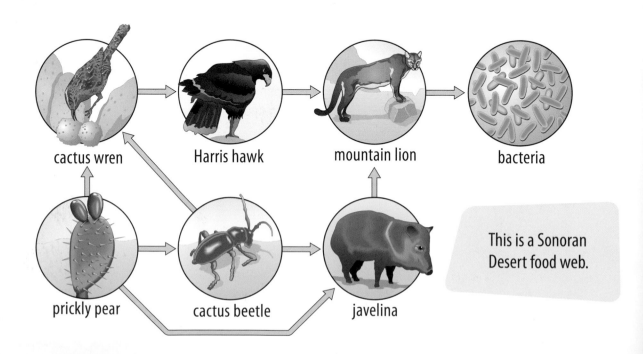

cactus wren   Harris hawk   mountain lion   bacteria

prickly pear   cactus beetle   javelina

This is a Sonoran Desert food web.

GOBI DESERT

The Gobi Desert is the largest Asian desert, covering parts of northern China and southern Mongolia. Temperatures in this cold desert plunge to –40°C (–40°F). The Himalaya Mountains block rain clouds from reaching the Gobi. This makes it very dry.

Scattered shrubs and grasses grow on the Gobi's gravel plains. **Nomadic** herders raise sheep, cattle, goats, and camels here. Wild animals like ibex and gazelles also roam the desert, **grazing** on shrubs, grasses, and lichens. Wolves and eagles hunt these desert grazers.

LOSING A LINK: THE BACTRIAN CAMEL

The Bactrian camel is **adapted** to live in the harsh Gobi Desert. Today it is one of the rarest **mammals** in the world. Only 1,000 of them survive in the wild. Their numbers have declined because of hunting and competition with domestic animals for grazing land and water. Oil and gold mining have also reduced their fragile **habitat**.

A Bactrian camel uses fat stored in its hump for **energy**.

SAHARA DESERT

The Sahara Desert covers most of North Africa. It is the world's largest desert. It stretches from the Atlantic Ocean in the west to the Red Sea in the east. About 2.5 million people live in this vast desert. Some are nomads who travel long distances with camels, goats, sheep, and donkeys.

The harsh climate of the Sahara makes it difficult for plants and animals to live there. Strong winds blow, causing sandstorms. The Sahara receives about 7.6 centimetres (3 inches) of rain a year. Some parts of the desert go without rain for many years.

Because it is so dry, parts of the Sahara have little plant life. There are vast sand dunes, gravel plains, and rocky mountains. Plants often grow near **oases**, or desert land with water.

Jumping desert rodents called jerboa are **primary consumers** in a Sahara food chain. Jerboa eat seeds, roots, and insects. Secondary consumers like the sand cat listen for the jerboa's high-pitched squeaks. The jerboa sometimes **hibernates** during the hottest months.

This food web shows how energy is transferred in the Sahara Desert.

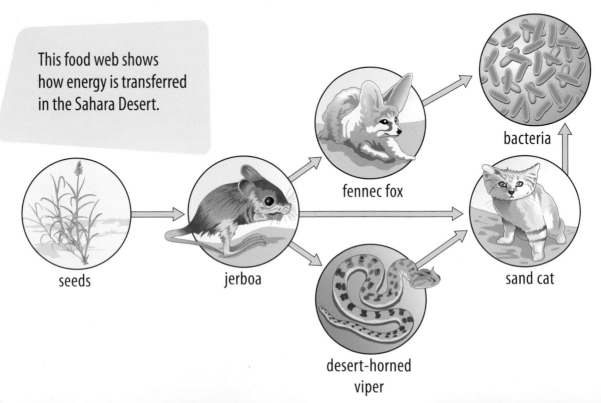

seeds

jerboa

fennec fox

bacteria

sand cat

desert-horned viper

Sand cats can be found in the African and Asian deserts. They have thick fur on their foot pads, which protects them from hot sand.

GREAT SANDY DESERT

One creature that has adapted well to the heat of the Sahara is the sand cat. This small cat has thick fur on its foot pads to protect it from the hot sand. It hunts at night for jerboa, vipers, and other animals.

Red sand dunes stretch for many kilometres in the Great Sandy Desert of north-west Australia. While the desert is dry for much of the year, **monsoon** rains fall during the wet season. After the rains, desert flowers bloom. Other producers include spinifex grass and desert shrubs and trees.

The bilby is a small **marsupial** that eats spinifex grass seeds. It scratches the soil to find desert ants, which it picks up with its long tongue. Secondary consumers like dingoes, foxes, lizards, and hawks prey on bilbies.

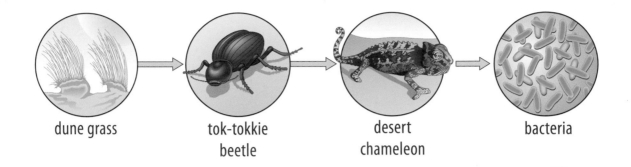

dune grass   tok-tokkie beetle   desert chameleon   bacteria

This food chain shows how energy is transferred in the Namib Desert.

NAMIB DESERT

Vast stretches of sand cover the Namib Desert in south-west Africa. The tallest sand dunes in the world are here, reaching over 300 metres (1,000 feet) high. The desert borders the Atlantic Ocean for about 1,600 kilometres (1,000 miles). Although the Namib receives very little rain, thick ocean fog rolls over the dunes. Plants and animals survive on water from the fog.

The desert's producers include welwitschia, a plant that can live for 2,500 years. Welwitschia grows two long leaves that absorb water from fog. The tok-tokkie beetle eats grass and seeds that are carried by the wind and collect in the dunes. Lizards and geckos feed on the beetles. Sidewinder snakes hunt lizards like the desert chameleon.

PATAGONIAN DESERT

The Patagonian Desert is a cold desert in South America. The average temperature is 1 to 3°C (33.8 to 37°F). Winter lasts for seven months of the year. Winter temperatures are cold enough for frost, but there is rarely enough moisture for snow. The Andes Mountains block moisture from the Pacific Ocean, keeping the region very dry. Strong dry winds blow across gravel plains and sandstone canyons.

Young guanaco graze on grasses and other plants.

The guanaco is a primary consumer here. It is the largest South American grazer and a member of the same family as camels. Guanaco live in small herds and graze on grasses and shrubs. When a mountain lion is near, guanaco can speed up to 56 kilometres (35 miles) per hour.

HOW ARE HUMANS HARMING DESERT FOOD CHAINS?

Almost one-quarter of Earth's surface is desert. Deserts include vast areas with bare soil and low-growing plants. Plants and animals that live in deserts must cope with extreme temperatures and little water. Despite these harsh conditions, many living things have **adapted** to survive in deserts. Some of the plants and animals that live in deserts are found in no other **habitats**.

People also live, work in, and visit deserts. About 500 million people, or 8 per cent of the world's population, live in or at the edges of deserts. In the past, people who lived in the desert made their living in one of three ways. Some were hunter-gatherers who collected desert plants and hunted wild animals. Others raised herds of animals such as camels, cattle, and sheep that **grazed** on desert grasses. Still others farmed in **oases** and along rivers.

Nomadic people travel across deserts, hunting and gathering food.

CHANGING USES OF DESERTS

Today, some of the ways humans live in and use the desert are changing. People who were once hunter-gatherers have settled. Some have become cattle ranchers. Dams have been built to supply water for people and their animals, and to make electricity. Farmland near rivers and oases suffers after these changes.

Cities have grown on the edges of deserts, bringing more people. Tourists also flock to deserts. Deserts have been mined for oil, gas, and minerals. Large military bases have been built in deserts. All of these uses require **energy**, roads, and water resources. The new ways people use deserts compete with the traditional ways. They also affect plants and animals that make up desert food chains.

Cities have grown on the edges of deserts, using scarce water and resources.

OVERGRAZING

Keeping too many domestic animals on dry land leads to **overgrazing**. Animals destroy desert grasses and other plants by eating them to the roots and trampling them. Without roots to hold soil in place, soil blows away. New plants cannot sprout. With fewer and fewer **producers**, desert **consumers** also decline.

Wild animals in deserts do not overgraze. When plants in one place become scarce, the animals move to another area. Then plants regrow. In the past, nomads moved sheep, goats, and cattle from place to place, so the land was not overgrazed.

Today, people are raising more animals in the desert. These animals are often kept on ranches. In the Chihuahuan Desert in the southern United States and Mexico, cattle graze on grasses and shrubs. They damage desert plants, especially along streams. Some of the streams are used for irrigation. Desert wildlife depends on streams for water and plants for food. It no longer survives in some areas because of cattle grazing. Dust from **eroding** soil also **pollutes** the air.

When cattle graze on desert ranches, there is little grass and water left for desert wildlife.

Mining for opals in South Australia has left this desert barren.

HABITAT DESTRUCTION

Copper, lead, salt, and other minerals are mined in deserts around the world. Mining uses huge amounts of water, leaving less water for plants and animals. Rivers and rain carry **toxic** chemicals from rubble left at mines. These **pollutants** can harm plants, wildlife, and people.

Human use damages the fragile desert surface. People race across sand dunes in off-road vehicles. Military vehicles also drive across deserts. Their tyres crush the thin desert **soil crust**, destroying plants and **decomposers**. Water cannot seep into **compacted** ground, and runs off. Plants do not sprout, and the soil erodes. Consumers find less food. It can take 100 years or more for the desert crust to form again.

Camels that were brought to Australia consume plants and drink scarce water.

ALIEN INVADERS

People sometimes bring animals and plants with them when they settle in new places. At other times, people carry seeds to new places by accident. The **alien species** compete with **native** plants and animals for water, space, and food. Native desert plants and animals sometimes have trouble surviving when aliens change their habitat.

Camels are not native to Australia. Ten thousand or more camels were brought from India between 1840 and 1907. The camels helped explorers in the Australian outback. Because camels are well adapted to desert life, their numbers increased. They could go without water for a long time, ate most desert plant species, and carried heavy loads. But over time roads, railways, and aeroplanes reached the desert. People no longer needed camels to do work. The camels became **feral**.

There are now close to one million feral camels in Australia. The camels compete with native animals for food and water, especially during drought.

CLIMATE CHANGE

Average temperatures around the globe have increased in the past 100 years. Human activity – especially burning coal, oil, and natural gas – has contributed to **global warming** and climate change. Desert temperatures are likely to continue to rise. Some deserts, such as the Gobi, might receive more rainfall. Other deserts, such as the Sahara, may become drier. There may be more dust storms in places with less rainfall.

The changes in temperature and rainfall will affect desert food chains. For example, scientists expect that nearly half of the bird, butterfly, and **mammal** species in the Chihuahuan Desert will be replaced by other animals by 2055. With new plants there may be more wildfires, damaging native desert plants. After wildfires soils often erode.

Dust storms occur when strong winds blow loose sand and dust from dry ground.

WHAT CAN YOU DO TO PROTECT DESERT FOOD CHAINS?

Plants, animals, and people have lived in deserts for thousands of years. Some of these plants and animals live nowhere else on Earth. They have **adapted** to life with little water.

Many people understand the value of deserts. Scientists study the amazing plants and animals that live there. Tourists visit deserts to see wild flowers and animals. Around the world, people are conserving (saving) deserts.

Plants and animals that live in sand dunes are protected in the Simpson Desert Conservation Park.

Conservation groups are working to save desert animals such as this elephant and rhinoceros in Namibia.

CONSERVING DESERTS

In Australia, many deserts are now part of the desert reserve system. Red sand dunes up to 37 metres (120 feet) high stretch across the Simpson Desert for hundreds of kilometres. These are some of the world's longest sand dunes. Spinifex grasslands provide food for 190 bird **species**, lizards, and small **marsupials** such as the mulgara. To preserve this desert, the Australian government set up Simpson Desert **Conservation** Park and Regional Reserve. Volunteers help to conserve the fragile landscape.

In Namibia conservation groups are working to save the black rhinoceros. In the 1980s, poaching (illegal hunting) almost caused the rhinoceros to die out. The Save the Rhino Trust was formed to stop poachers. Now the rhinoceros population has grown again.

The Namibian government and conservation groups are working together to create a new national park. The park will protect a 6-million-hectare (15-million-acre) area where rhinoceroses and other wildlife **migrate** through the Namib Desert. It will link two other national parks. By protecting the rhino's **habitat**, the park will protect many other plants and animals in the desert food chain.

HELPING HUMANS

Desert plants and animals may hold the key to solving serious human problems. As more people live in **arid** regions, getting enough fresh water is a concern. We can learn how to collect and conserve water by studying desert **organisms**. In order to learn from them, we must protect them and their habitats.

The tok-tokkie beetle of the Namib Desert collects water in one of the driest places on Earth. At night, this beetle climbs to the top of a dune and raises its rear end into the wind. Fog **condenses** on special bumps on its back and runs into its mouth. After studying this beetle, scientists designed water-collecting devices. They made plastic sheets that are just like the beetle's bumps. The sheets can condense water from fog. By learning about desert animals, scientists found a way to help humans collect water in the desert. What else might we learn from desert organisms?

This man holds a tok-tokkie beetle in a nature reserve in Namibia. It is important for humans to keep learning about desert organisms.

This volunteer helps picks up litter in a desert in the US.

CLEANING UP THE DESERT

Thirteen-year-old Cameron Oliver from Abu Dhabi was upset when he found out that camels in the desert were dying after eating plastic and other litter. He decided to try and make people aware of the effects of desert litter. First, he learned more about the problem. He visited a scientist who had researched the effects of plastic. Cameron learned that wind blows litter from villages and cities into the desert. It lands in the sand, where camels and other animals nibble it. Young camels choke and die on the plastic. When an older camel swallows the plastic, it blocks their **intestine** (an organ that helps animals digest food), and eventually kills them.

First, Cameron put up a display about the problem at his school. He let people know what they could do to stop harming camels. Newspapers and radio and TV interviews covered his work to stop littering.

TOP 10 THINGS YOU CAN DO TO PROTECT DESERTS

There are lots of things you can to do help protect desert **habitats** and the animals that live in them. Here is a list of the top 10:

1 Learn about desert plants and animals and teach others about them. The more people know about deserts, the more they will want to conserve them.

2 Be a good desert visitor. Stay on roads or trails. Do not drop litter that could harm wildlife.

3 Let other people know that riding off-road in lorries, motorcycles, and mountain bikes harms the desert.

4 Enjoy looking at or taking pictures of desert plants and animals, but do not disturb them.

5 Water is very scarce in deserts. When people use water in and near deserts, there is less clean water left for plants and animals. Conserve water in your home. Fix leaky taps. Turn off the water when you brush your teeth. Take short showers instead of baths.

6 Save water in your garden. Collect water in a water butt and use it to water plants. Plant **native** flowers that do not need watering.

7 Plant a native tree. Trees provide shade and make your home cooler, so you need less air conditioning. Trees also store carbon dioxide. Carbon dioxide causes **global warming**.

8 Ride a bike or walk to a friend's house instead of asking for a lift. You will save petrol. A lot of petrol comes from wells in deserts.

9 Donate time and money to **conservation** groups that are helping to save habitats.

10 Write to local and national officials, telling them that you support laws to conserve deserts.

GLOSSARY

adapt when a species undergoes changes that help it survive

adaptation special structures or behaviours that make an organism well suited to its environment

alien animal or plant that is brought by people to a new environment

arid dry; lacking rainfall

bacterium (plural **bacteria**) tiny living decomposer found everywhere

carcass dead body of an animal

carnivore animal that eats only other animals

cellulose material found in the cell walls of plants

compact packed closely together

condense change from water vapour (gas) to liquid water

conservation protecting and saving the natural environment

consumer organism that eats other organisms

decomposer organism that breaks down and gets nutrients from dead plants and animals and their waste

endangered at risk of dying out

energy power needed to grow, move, and live

enzyme protein that speeds up a chemical reaction

eroding wearing away of rocks and soil by wind, water, ice, or chemicals

evaporation process of losing liquid to the air as water vapour

extinct kind of animal that is no longer in existence

feral animal or plant in a wild state that was once owned or used by humans

fungus (plural **fungi**) decomposer organism including mushrooms, toadstools, and their relatives

global warming worldwide increase in air and ocean temperature

graze eat grass and other green plants in a field or meadow

habitat place where an organism lives

herbivore animal that eats plants

hibernate to be inactive during winter months, when there is little food

intestine tube in body that carries and processes food

mammal warm-blooded animal that produces milk to feed its young

marsupial mammal that has a pouch where young are carried and fed

migrate to move from one area to another

monsoon season of heavy rainfall

GLOSSARY

native plant or animal that lives in the place where it evolved

nectar sugary substance made by plants to attract pollinators

nutrient substance that a living thing needs to live and grow

nomadic moving from place to place and not having a fixed home

oasis (plural **oases**) desert land with water

omnivore animal that eats plants and other animals

organism living thing

overgrazing destroying plants by eating them down to the roots and trampling them

photosynthesis process that plants use to turn energy from the Sun into food and oxygen

pleated folded

pollen small grains that are the male part of a flower. Pollen combines with the female part of the flower to form seeds.

pollinator animal that carries pollen from the male part of a flower to the female part

pollutant harmful chemical that is released into the air, water, or soil

pollute release harmful waste into the land, air, or water

predator animal that hunts and eats other animals

prey animal that is eaten by another animal; also, when an animal pursues another animal to eat it

primary consumer animal that eats plants

producer organism (plant) that can make its own food

scavenger organism that feeds on dead plants, animals, and their waste

secondary consumer animal that eats other animals

soil crust living layer of microscopic organisms and plants in desert soils

species type of plant or animal

tap root main root of a plant that grows straight down from the stem

toxic poisonous

FIND OUT MORE

BOOKS

Essential Habitats: Desert Habitats, Paul Bennett (Tick Tock Media, 2009)

Focus on Habitats: Desert Animals, Steven Savage (Hodder Wayland, 2006)

Geographywise: Deserts, Leon Grey (Hodder Wayland, 2010)

Kingfisher Young Knowledge: Deserts, Nicola Davies (Kingfisher Books, 2007)

WEBSITES

www.alicespringsdesertpark.com.au/kids/plants/index.shtml
Learn more about Australia's Alice Springs Desert Park.

www.desertmuseum.org/kids/oz/
Learn more about the Sonora Desert at the Arizona-Sonora Desert Museum's website.

http://savetherhinotrust.org/
Learn about efforts to save the rhino and other desert wildlife in Namibia.

www.greatestplaces.org/fauna/fauna.html/basebeetle.html
Watch the tok-tokkie beetle in Namibia collect water from fog on a sand dune.

www.cameronscamelcampaign.com/
Learn how a 13-year-old boy living in Abu Dhabi, in the United Arab Emirates, set out to clean up litter in the desert, and protect camels and wildlife.

FURTHER RESEARCH

Choose a topic from this book you'd like to research further. Do you live near a desert you would like to know more about? Or is there a faraway desert you think is exotic? Was there a creature in this book you find interesting? Is there something harming desert food chains you'd like to know more about putting a stop to? Visit your local library to find out more information.

INDEX